The New You
How to Create Your Own Reality
Second Edition

G. Michael Vasey

For Paul, Liam, Jon and Denisa

And if I have not sufficient greatness of soul to strive to become the Master of Nature, overthrow the Elements, hold communion with Supreme Intelligences, command demons, become the father of giants, create new worlds, speak with God upon his formidable Throne, and compel the Cherubim who guards the gate of terrestrial Paradise to let me stroll now and then in its alleyways, it is I, and I alone, who am to blame or to be pitied.

Comte De Gabalis, by Abbe N. de Montfaucon de Villars

Table of Contents

Introduction

As you read these words, your eyes are taking in light emitted from the computer screen or that are reflected back from the page. This light enters your eye and is converted into electrical signals, which are sent to a part of your brain that processes them back into a picture. The picture is upside down, by the way, but your brain then presents the page's picture to your consciousness the right way up despite this.

The image that you see is 'created' inside your brain. It is more or less the same processes at work, that gives you the feeling being transmitted from the nerves in your bum that it is rather numb from sitting on that seat. It is just a set of electrical signals sent to the brain where they are presented to your consciousness. Think about this a bit more, and at the same time, realize that you are just a cloud of atoms within a larger cloud of atoms. Even your brain is simply just a cloud of atoms.

What is reality? Is your reality, the one created inside your brain, different to mine? When we both 'see' the color purple, are we even seeing the same hue or color? We are trained to know that that particular set of vibrations is to be described as 'purple.'

Quantum physics (don't go away, I won't bore you with too much detail) has been trying to unravel reality for quite some time now, and what physicists have discovered is simply mind-boggling. The brain is presented with much more information than you can actually use, so it dumbs it down for you. It actually chooses which information to present to your consciousness, and it does so just moments after what you are observing actually took place. Imagine that! And think about this—what information is it choosing *not* to present to your consciousness? What is the filter that it uses to decide what information to present to you?

In fact, everything is vibration; or, put in a more scientific way, it is all waves of different wavelengths. Quantum physics shows that waves can be particles and particles can be waves. The decider of whether wave or particle is the observer—you. The act of observing by a consciousness actually 'collapses the waveform' into particles.

What does this mean? It means that you continuously create your reality and that you interact with all the other co-creators of reality as you do this amazing feat. Yes, it is all a sort of matrix, and that is a fact. How you feel, how you are raised, how you speak, what you say, what you think, and a myriad other inputs, determine your filter and therefore your reality from moment to moment.

Imagine what you could do if you were truly a conscious being and not operating more or less on autopilot much of the time? Maybe you could make things change via the force of your will and imagination. It's all about your imagination, you know. Maybe it isn't so much faith that can move mountains as it is about imagination and having faith in that imagining. If you have come across 'cosmic ordering' or The Secret, then you have been exposed to a rather crude and materialistic form of this concept. It is, by the way, no secret. It has been well known by occultists and magicians for thousands of years.

Reality - What Is It?

In esoteric circles, there is the concept that there is both a reality and an actuality. Reality is essentially what <u>you</u> can perceive of the actuality, and this actuality cannot be directly perceived. Reality is seen as fundamentally a self-made and self-sustained illusion colored by your filters and the strength of your imagination.

We don't really know what actuality is. It's a cloud of atoms and particles I suppose, and scientists tell us that it is mostly space. It is also energy, but why it is and what it really is, we don't actually know. Perhaps it is the mind of God; perhaps it is just a computer simulation that we exist in, like the Sims. We don't know. We can only postulate, theorize and dream.

Reality—your reality—is created using your imagination and your belief system. Your culture, upbringing, beliefs and the rules by which you now live your life all go into filtering and creating that reality. The reality in which you live is something created inside your brain, inside your mind. Yes, you have six senses to interact with the outer world but think about that. If I touch something, do I really feel it? No, I don't. I receive a bunch of signals and impulses in my brain, and this is processed to give me the idea that I felt something. In actuality, a bunch of atoms somehow moved towards another bunch of atoms, but in my mind, I touched something that I recognize as, say, a wooden table.

In order to build up our picture of reality, we need to be able to visualize colors, objects, sounds and so on. We need to build a database of these in our heads that we can compare things to and recognize what it is we 'see.' But all of this—every image, sounds and sensation—takes place in only your mind. You were taught that this is wood, this is metal, this is a tree, and this is a face and so on.

You were told what you should see and what you should not. You were conditioned by your parents, school and life experiences. Your culture told you what was acceptable and what was not. It helped you to create the reality that you then spend the rest of your life trapped in. If you understand this, then just like Neo in The Matrix, you realize we have a choice. Do you want to wake up?

Your reality is actually just an illusion—a wakeful dream. It is not actuality. Each and every one of us falls into the trap of believing in our own reality even though we are creating that reality moment-to-moment through our belief set and our imagination. As a result, the world looks exactly like you expect it to.

Let's examine that statement philosophically for a moment, shall we? If you believe that the world is a cruel place filled with hate, then that is what it is; conversely, if you see a paradise filled with beautiful people, then that is also what you get. The problem is that most of us simply stumble through our lives out of control in terms of our thought processes, thinking things more or less spontaneously. One minute, the world is a cruel place full of hate, and the next, it can be a paradise filled with beautiful people. In other words, we are continually sending out mixed signals. As a result, the reality that we create is, as we say in Yorkshire, 'neither nowt nor summat.' We fail to create our reality with any consistency.

Magic and Reality

I have made an effort to study magical and occult systems over the years, and in the process, I have come to some startling conclusions. You see, the only difference between a 'magician' and an ordinary person is that a magician makes conscious efforts to create a better reality moment-by-moment; whereas a non-magician simply goes with the flow—taking inputs without question and creating a reality that is based on non-conscious direction. They sleep through their lives in a cocoon of their own making.

But studying and practicing magic involves a great deal of self-examination and introspection, as well as a lot of practice of thought discipline and control. It also aims to build and enhance your imaginative faculties. In essence, right there you have several of the keys to creating reality.

- We must be consistent and willful in setting up what is it is that we want to create,

- We must remain disciplined and focused on that objective, unwavering in its pursuit,

- We must also have the clarity of mind to stay focused and a powerful imagination to actually see and feel it around us,

- We must know ourselves and be in tune with our Higher Self in order to align what we think we want with what we actually need.

If we can do all of this and do it willfully and purposely then I believe that we can and do create reality by magic. (I am also pretty sure that one day, science will come to the same conclusions.)

Now, before you discount me as a strange dreamer, I want you to think about a few things that tend to suggest this really is how it works:

1. Certain psychological techniques proven to have an impact and used by sports people and others, use the concept of strongly visualizing a result along with the bodily training to achieve that result. Athletes already use a form of this magic to achieve. They become so focused

and so willful about their imagining and visualizing performance goals that, in some instances, they actually achieve their objectives,

2. Every book that I have ever read about positive thinking and creating success, all teach aspects of this same approach that involves imagination, acting out, will, mindfulness, assuming that it will happen, being grateful and thankful for it and so on. They all use similar techniques. They use magic. Where they fall short, in my opinion, is that they forget to emphasize the knowing yourself part; and, trust me, this is their weakness,

3. I also happen to think that aspects of quantum physics seem to be pointing in a similar direction. We create our own reality, and if we just knew how to do it properly, and if we could do it without ego, out of love, that reality would be heaven on Earth. It would be Nirvana. But it would be our Nirvana, as I also believe that each of us has the potential to create something slightly different. Unique. It is this that divides us and separates us and yet it enriches us. It affords us an ability to co-create endless parallel worlds of Nirvanas.

Be Like a Child Again

Children will often bring a smile to our lips because their worldview is unfettered by outside influences and devoid of any political pressures or opinions. Their innocence often provides us with laughter and sometimes remarkably powerful, but simple, insights into our complex world.

I have played more than my part in terms of aiding this phenomenon having fathered four children to date, and each and every one of them has taught me something valuable or brought a smile to my face in terms of what they did or said. All kids are different right from the very beginning. Having watched my twin boys grow up, I can say that they are different from the very first second of life outside the womb and probably from even before that. Obviously, it is my youngest child who now alone has this childlike ability to point out glitches in the matrix as my three sons are now all grown and have already lost their childlike innocence.

This childlike innocence and confidence might not seem like very much, but if you think about it, if thoughts have the power to create reality, then why do we not always get exactly what we want?

The answer to that question is because no matter how much we try to convince ourselves that we are thinking positively and believing completely, we also know that we are not. As adults, we have been told so many times that we *can't* or that we *shouldn't* that it has become an inbuilt mechanism to ensure our failure. We are programmed to fail.

I start out all positive and confident that my thoughts are of best-selling books or a vacation in Mexico. I am sure that this will happen if I just keep picturing it, believing in it and seeing it. A couple of hours later though, it starts.

"Don't be bloody daft," says that initial, passing, doubting thought.

Internal bickering, doubt, and ultimately, failure follow this. The child, however, has yet to be programed for failure in quite the same way. The child still knows how to believe without self-doubt and ought to be able to actually create their reality.

The Power of Thought

Your thoughts are powerful. Your thoughts create. <u>Your thoughts are things</u>.

Some would argue that thoughts actually do create in what is often termed the 'astral plane'—a sort of substratum of thoughts and ideas on which the physical world around us is based. If this is true, then what do you think about? What sort of mental world are you creating?

The problem is that we are deeply impacted by the outside world and the external influences that help to govern and direct our thoughts. We often do not create our reality, but rather someone else's reality, instead. Watch the news, read a newspaper—it's all doom and gloom. It is all stories of war, famine, violence, global warming and terrorism, to name a few things. We can't help but ponder on these, think about them—even worry about them. We become fear-based people, and we lose our ability to create.

Taking Control

If you take a look at CNN's front page today or any day, you would be forgiven for being afraid. I really believe that the constant creation of fear by the media is a deliberate ploy to keep us trapped and locked up in a reality we don't want or deserve.

I am unafraid and totally convinced that everything is exactly as <u>it should be</u>.

No. I **will not** be afraid. Not now and not ever. Nor should you be. Instead, let's understand that everything is as it should be and that there is nothing to fear except that we will be corralled like dumb beasts into some place we don't wish to be if we let them.

The Need to Meditate

We all need to take time out and become silent. We should, in the silence of meditation, ponder on what we think about and why. Do we dream great things for the World and ourselves, or do we sink into deep, dark fear?

Take that time, and after meditating on what you think about and how you are influenced by fear mongers, start to try to build a different vision. Try to visualize a different world and a different you. Fill that world with light and see yourself being happy, carefree and having an abundance of gifts.

I believe that if more people meditated on the positives in life, two things would occur: First, we would create a better world for ourselves; and second, we would gradually escape from the clutches of fear. We would learn to actually live and reach our potential as humans and 'block' out all those negative influences.

Giving Attention

In a recent radio interview, I found myself talking about the idea that if we give a thing our attention, then it becomes real. In so many words, I was saying that we create our own reality through mental focus. You can, in fact, more or less prove this to yourself any time that you wish. Simply, think of something—something as bizarre as you want—and give it your focus. For example, decide that today you will see a mouse dance. Keep on giving this thought your focus and attention throughout the day—keep looking for that dancing mouse. I guarantee that you will, at some point during the day, see a dancing mouse even if it is just a Disney cartoon on TV.

If you experiment like this for a while, you come to the conclusion that one of two things is going on:

1. You are actually creating reality using thought, or

2. By focusing your attention on something, you are noticing it. It was always there, but you never registered it until the point that you gave it your focus.

Now, ask yourself this: Is there actually any difference in the two statements above? We simply cannot know whether we created that reality or whether we simply started to notice something that was there anyway; and, for us, it is essentially the same thing.

In magical training, we are taught, and we practice mental discipline and how to use our imaginative capacities. By learning to meditate for endless minutes with an empty mind or imagining that there is actually a matchbox on the table in front of you, we are training our mind to give attention to whatever we want to give our attention to. We may even use some tools to aid our imagination and mental focus in the form of ritual objects. We may even use a ritual to turn our attention onto something. There are many techniques, but all are really down to one thing—focus or attention.

I said earlier that thoughts are things. Well, what if I told you that energy follows thought? If I give my attention to something, then I give it energy, and I animate it and give it meaning in my life.

So, what if I could give something my proper focus and attention? After all, am I not simply a stream of consciousness and is it not the job of consciousness to focus attention and observe? *Faith can move mountains,* it is said. Faith is nothing but giving something attention and knowing that in doing so, whatever I wish will transpire.

So what if today, we gave some attention to our world? What if we all decided to focus our attention on the wonderful, the amazing, and miracle of life on Earth? What if we all sought out the good news and gave that our focus and attention?

Shall we try?

Expectation

The other day, I was participating in a discussion on Facebook. The theme of the topic was the supermarkets in the city that I live in in the Czech Republic, and one person posted a very long tirade about empty shelves. I was amazed. Empty shelves? Where? When?

This was so opposite to my own experiences with Brno supermarkets that I responded rather too quickly. I said something like, "You must live in a parallel universe..." Not knowing me, that comment was taken the wrong way, but I actually meant it. To me, this was another example of magic at work. We get what we expect. This person plainly had an expectation contrary to mine—that the supermarket shelves were often empty, and, as a result, they were. On the other hand, my expectations are that supermarkets are well stocked, and, for me, they are.

We all live in our own realities, and we reflect back what we expect. It's not quite that simple, of course, but in a nutshell, he sees the empty shelves of his own making, and I see the full shelves of my making. It's the glass half-empty or half-full thing, isn't it? Who would have thought I would be the half-full person?

You see, people are caught up in their self-constrained belief systems, torturing themselves and those around them, whereas, others live life full of expectation and optimism. You see people willingly being negative and walking around creating the little cloud above them. Of course, the Matrix is full of influencers and motivators that play on, feed, and drive these realities.

It all might be simple to manage if it was just you or I, but the real fun comes in how we interact and how our little realities impinge upon others. Your problems become mine and so on—if I let them. We create our own realities, but we are influenced by the collective drivers (fear, sex, wealth, love, hate, etc.), and, at the same time, interact with the realities of those around us. Surround yourself with happy people. Trust me. It's the way to go.

How we create that reality is as much about our upbringing, cultural origins and so on—the collective we are a part of—as anything else. To see the world differently, we have to escape that collective for another and another and another, until suddenly it becomes clear... I am having my creativity dictated to me. It is then that we look inwards for the truth. We get glimpses of that truth, and what we see is truly shocking. Rather than purposeful, willful beings creating a meaningful reality, we are robots, slaves or sheep (pick your term) working to help others create their reality!

To get to this point, we have to go through some personal pain because we have to reject so many things that we once accepted and believed to be the truth. Stripping away the chains of bondage and layers of control is painful, both to us and to those around us who just don't get it and who see their comfortable reality threatened by ours. We often end up alone, apart and isolated. But then we understand that we have to interact. We have to replace the collective drivers for everyone else as well as ourselves. The only way to do that is to interact, experience life, have compassion, be grateful and step forward in self-mastery. A very difficult if not impossible mandate, but not one that has been unknown. Take a look at these extracts from the Gospel of Thomas, for example.

> *"Let him who seeks continue seeking until he finds. When he finds, he will become troubled. When he becomes troubled, he will be astonished, and he will rule over the All."*

"If those who lead you say to you, 'See, the kingdom is in the sky,' then the birds of the sky will precede you. If they say to you, 'It is in the sea,' then the fish will precede you. Rather, the kingdom is inside of you, and it is outside of you. When you come to know yourselves, then you will become known, and you will realize that it is you who are the sons of the living father. But if you will not know yourselves, you dwell in poverty and it is you who are that poverty."

"Recognize what is in your sight, and that which is hidden from you will become plain to you. For there is nothing hidden which will not become manifest."

His disciples questioned him and said to him, "Do you want us to fast? How shall we pray? Shall we give alms? What diet shall we observe?" Jesus said, "Do not tell lies, and do not do what you hate, for all things are plain in the sight of heaven. For nothing hidden will not become manifest, and nothing covered will remain without being uncovered."

Prayer

A few years ago, some money was sent to me from the USA. The money should have arrived by Wednesday. On Thursday, it had still not arrived, and I began to worry that perhaps it had got lost. Modern banking isn't reliable, and they do make mistakes. About every four months, my money goes missing. It vaporizes into thin air between the US and the Czech Republic, and none of the banks will ever admit that it is their fault or that they know where my money is. Usually, it either eventually arrives or it ends up back in the originating account in the USA. The problem is that as soon as the money isn't there, I begin to expect that the banks have yet again screwed it up. This time, however, I decided I wasn't going to let that happen. My remedy was to pray. Yes—pray.

I sat and I focused my mind. God is everywhere, all-knowing and all-seeing. I thanked the all-knowing, all-seeing Deity for my blessings and then asked that my money show up the next day. I pictured the money sitting in my account. I visualized my money being in my bank account when I checked it online the next morning. I made myself believe that there was no possible way for it not to be there. There was not a shadow of a doubt in my mind, since the Deity is all seeing, all knowing and all-powerful, there was nothing else to do but confidently wait until the next day. The money was, of course, there.

This is how prayer works. This is how magic works, and this is how we create reality.

Perhaps a good example of this is when you simply know something is so. There are times when I know that my home soccer team, Hull City, will win or lose or draw. I don't mean I fancy a win or a loss; I mean I KNOW. I am always right in these instances without fail. The KNOWING is the faith in an outcome so strong that no other outcome is possible. None.

Prayer is a key part of life and of creating our lives. Proper prayer cannot fail to produce results. Proper prayer involves visualization, and it can be a wilful act of magic. Prayer should be a conversation with the Creator that begins with thanks and gratitude. Give it a try. It works.

Imagination

Imagination these days is undervalued. Kids no longer really need to exercise their imaginative faculties as it's all laid on a plate for them in video games, movies that leave nothing to the imagination and

TV. Yes, we had movies and TV growing up, , but they still needed the support of an active imagination. Our TV was in black and white until I was in my early teens and so you had to fill in the missing details for yourself. Special effects were pretty naff too and required imagination. Rather than play video games, I read books—a powerful tool to enhance your imagination. The human race is essentially being gently but surely relieved of its need for an imagination. I wonder if there is a motive behind this.

Imagination (and I don't mean daydreaming here, but the power of the mind to create images) is the key to magic. Yes, I know many of you do not believe in magic and think me a rather bizarre old mystic whom you nicely humor when he talks about magic, but you are sadly wrong. That we do create our reality I think these days is factual. You can Google how the brain functions and how, in fact, our mind creates the images, smells, sounds and so on that we sense. You can discover in physics how the reality we live in is mostly nothingness between particles, and yet somehow, our mind makes things seem solid. I could go on, but I won't. Reality exists only inside your head, and what actually 'is' is so strange, it is best not to think about it too hard.

Thoughts are things, too. I hear you laughing, but, seriously, thoughts are things and with enough, shall we say energy or the right type, they can manifest as your reality. To be honest, given that what you perceive doesn't actually exist anyway—aren't you living in a make believe world of thought forms? Look at the wall. Actually, it's just a bunch of atoms and is largely open space, and yet it seems solid to you. It's an image created in your mind, isn't it? So, if you could imagine—imagine so well you could actually see it—what would happen? In essence, you are already imagining a wall of a certain color, so have fun and imagine it a different color. If you are good at imagining, it will appear the color you imagine. So there you go… Do you begin to understand why imagination is so important?

What we see, hear and believe was taught to us. In essence, reality is a sort of preferred long-utilized imagined version of actuality, isn't it? So, who told you to see the world you see? In part, the very same people who are robbing us of our ability to escape from their desired version of reality right now—all around us, all the time.

If you strip down a system of magic, it comes down to two things:

        1. Imagination
        2. Energy

By the way, the neat thing is that you even have to imagine the energy!

Magic is the ability to change reality at will. Imagination is the tool and will (or energy) is the power to do it.

Don't believe in magic? You should. You work magic involuntarily every second of every day. Want to gain control of YOUR life? Learn how to really imagine, visualize and dream.

The World We Live In

The decline of the expert opinion and its believability parallels in many ways the decline in respect for experience and the aged. Instead, we appear to have become a society fed a constant diet of myth and half-baked theory because we are gullible enough to believe it.

Once upon a time, society respected its elders. With many decades of life experience, we valued their wisdom gained over those years. Not anymore. Old people are, well, old, smelly, slow and stupid. Who wants to listen to them? It works similarly with expertise, except in this case; the expert is biased, bought and rigid in their thinking and not to be trusted.

The problem with this is, if I may be blunt, humanity is in decline going around and around in ever-decreasing circles on its way to destination stupidity. Once, many childhood diseases were largely a thing of the past. Then someone with an agenda decided inoculation was responsible for a myriad of issues. Out on social media it goes, and now… all these terrible diseases are back, and many parents will argue until they're blue in the face that they read or heard that vaccinating your child is a bad thing to do. Even if their doctor tells them the opposite, they would rather believe what they read or what their neighbor told them. They are being lied to, and they believe it.

This is just one example, but there are many, many others.

Let's be clear. I am not sanctioning belief for the sake of belief here. Asking questions is always good. Getting a good education around any issue that worries or interests you is also good, but the source should count for something. People with years of experience and expertise through learning got there because they cared to. Their viewpoint is of more value than the blogger who writes with a lot of angst, but no actual knowledge.

Social media is a good thing in many respects, but it is helping to strengthen a decline in critical thinking. Memes and stories get passed around, and somehow people are gullible enough to believe the most ridiculous of stories. If an expert suggests that these stories are, in fact, nonsense, they are verbally insulted and bullied. We no longer value expertise that education brings nor the wisdom that comes with age. Instead, somehow, we place more value on going with the crowd—that nebulous, often anonymous, mass of people who have no expertise and little wisdom. Could it be that our ego wants us to believe that we really are experts and can make good decisions on everything? Do we dislike experts and expertise?

Would you really hire me to do your plumbing and not listen to me on matters involving geology with my Ph.D. in geology?

If this trend continues, there are troubled times ahead. You see, in accepting other people's desires for reality, we reject our own; and we become sheep helping to sustain another reality altogether. Instead, be a critical thinker and create your own reality. Sheep are easy to manipulate. Critical thinkers are not.

Just recently, someone called me a 'denier'. I suddenly found myself thinking about the things we call people – the words that we use and how we use them. It struck me that these are words of power. Words like 'sexist', 'racist', denier' and so on. They carry a weight and a magical intent that has been placed there by the intent of the many times those words have been used. They are in a way a sort of egregore (an occult concept representing a "thoughtform" or "collective group mind", an autonomous psychic entity made up of, and influencing, the thoughts of a group of people.) in a word.

Let me return to the word 'denier' as in climate change denier. When someone uses this expression against you it has the desired effect of belittling, but perhaps more importantly, it effectively destroys the expertise of the person being called a denier. You become just another 'foolish' person who denies the 'truth' of climate change. It stops any further useful conversation with its negativity and simplicity. It carries the weight of popular opinion against the person it is being used against. It has become a magical word with magical results for the negative.

The same with many of these words. Once you call someone a racist – they are one in effect with all the utter negativity that invokes. You have summoned the weight of the word in common usage and essentially sent off a negative magical arrow that encumbers the person termed such. Now there are racists and there are sexists – don't get me wrong. What I am trying to say is that these words have become part of the lexicon of avoiding debate and of shifting someone from a probably reasonable position into one of defensive argument. You can use these words to do immense damage to someone who is not a racist or a sexist or whatever word is used.

I throw this thought out there…. maybe I'm wrong but I feel in today's world, this is about creating a negative brand or an attempt to destroy a personal brand or reputation. One of the first things I learned as a marketing executive was how to destroy or at least eat away at the competitor's credibility by using certain negative phrases or words. However, when these words are used over and over, they take on an occult power that can have – and is meant to have – damaging impacts.

When someone in a discussion on climate change calls you a denier, they shift the whole conversation through the weight of that word. It doesn't matter what expertise you may have, whether in fact you are expressing a doubt about an aspect of climate change – nope. It robs you of credibility, robs you of your expertise and reputation and it puts you down.

The Truth

We hear these two important little words quite often. There are all types and kinds of truths, and many of us spend our lives seeking truth.

A favourite saying of mine is, *"The older I get, the less I think I know about anything."* Another way to say this would be that the older I get, the less I am certain of any truth—at least in the absolute sense. I don't know what I am or what my purpose is. I don't know what the Universe is nor its purpose—if there even is one. If there were, would I comprehend it? These are the questions that I ask and the answers I seek in vain. Perhaps we all do?

In recent years, due mostly to social media, I have come to understand that people do not share truth; rather, they all have their own versions of it. For conspiracy theorists, as one extreme, there is a version of the truth, and I think for religious zealots who will happily blow themselves and others up, there plainly is a version of the truth, too.

I often wonder if, in fact, people's truths are reality. What if we all shared a framework of a Universe in which multiple shades of overlapping reality were possible depending on the observer's outlook? In fact, there are a lot of brighter people than me in the scientific community who suggest that we live in a hologram or computer program. The substrate of this hologram is created by the observer's expectations and thoughts. Yes, you have heard it from me before—we create our own reality. What I am saying is that truth, if there truly is any such thing, is part of our *expectations* and *mindset*. It is therefore surely something we ourselves create, and why could it not be that our truths are all true to some degree because we make them so? Perhaps there isn't one reality here, but a multitude of marginally overlapping realities that we are cognizant of depending on how we wish to see the world?

What this would mean is that the conspiracy theorist is right, and so am I when I think he is nuts for seeing conspiracy everywhere.
It would also mean that how I think and how I choose to see things is critically important. The 'know thyself' aspect of magic and the seeking of balance then becomes a compass that points to truth— perhaps absolute truth. If we never understand ourselves and never perceive balance, then truth is always relative and relative only to us. The magician then is a true seeker of truth as opposed to the religious person who is essentially setting their compass to point to someone else's version of the truth so that it becomes a shared, but still relative, truth.

These ponderings made me check out where the word truth actually comes from. I wasn't surprised to learn that the word TRUTH derives from the word 'true.' In turn, the word true originates from the proto-German for having good faith. To quote from Wikipedia,

"...thus, 'truth' involves both the quality of 'faithfulness, fidelity, loyalty, sincerity, veracity', and that of 'agreement with fact or reality', in Anglo-Saxon expressed by sōþ (Modern English sooth)."

I rest my case.

Perhaps truth, though, is something that's actually only true for you?

I have spent much of my life seeking the truth; and now, not only have I yet to find the truth, I am no longer sure the truth actually exists. Here is why.

Firstly, each of us has a sort of core of beliefs—things that we have been told are correct. This core is nurtured by our parents and then the educational system that teach us either what they accept as truth or what that they were taught as being truth and they have found nothing better to replace it with. Some things we are taught may be closer to the truth than others in that 'two plus two equals four' seems like truth, whereas something like 'margarine is good for you' is an opinion masquerading as truth. And so, it goes with pretty much everything you think you are and that you believe in. It is not so much truth as conditioning—an acceptable version or interpretation of reality.

When we get a bit older, we start to think for ourselves. Or do we? In fact, we don't really think for ourselves because very rarely do we challenge what we had already been taught. We simply sharpen the set of thinking and analysis tools we had been given by the programming we experienced growing up. Peer pressure and the choices we make about who we mix with, what we read, what we do and so on influence our development of who we are, but for most people who don't drift so far from the security and safety of the familiar, the challenges are hardly viewpoint-changing. They are more likely small wrinkles of personal differences.

Everything that you believe you are and that you think you know is most probably a lie. You deceive yourself if you think it is truth because it can only be, at best, a version of someone's truth. Probably not yours but more likely, societies' truth.

There may come a time when you start to really inquire and begin to meditate and focus on that core that you believe to be you. If you persist in this approach, it is possible that you will conclude as I have done that you do not know who you really are and that much of your life has been about living to expectations rather than to your inner will and those expectations. They were almost always someone else's expectations, not yours. It is quite a shock when you understand this, but there is still no truth. Rather, there is the realization that everything outside of you is an illusion—it is Maya. You begin to conclude that in order to see the outside world with a hint of the truth, you first need to find out who you really are.

Now, here, I am going to digress a little bit so bear with me, please.

Stepping back from this brink, I can hear you saying, *"But I know truth. I see it with my own eyes and hear it with my own ears."* No, actually you really don't. Do me a favor and Google about how good we are at observation, and you will be amazed at how poor a skill this is for most people. You see a crime or an accident? You see your version of it, and someone else who saw the same thing at the same time might disagree with your version of events. Did the man really have black hair? Was he really of athletic build? The details of what you observe are part actual observation and a lot of your brain filling in the gaps based on… yes, what you believe and have been programmed with. So, actually, you don't see or hear the truth, but just an imperfect interpretation of it—your interpretation.

We also have an amazing capacity to deny the truth. Our memory is selective, too. Not only did I interpret what I saw and heard, but also, I may even have selectively remembered to reinforce my interpretation. The act of remembering actually alters the memory itself. Just be honest with yourself for a moment—how many memories have you altered deliberately to suit your viewpoint?

So, you see, truth—absolute truth—cannot actually exist; or rather, we cannot grasp it. If the truth stared us in the face, we would probably miss it and interpret it somehow in alignment with our ego and our belief system. Truth is like reality in this respect.

This is how people can fundamentally disagree over things. This is how we are exploited, too. The media, the politicians, the religious leaders—they exploit us and manipulate 'truth.' Why do you read the Telegraph or the Daily Mirror? Most likely because you agree with how they interpret events. There is a shared view of the truth. But beware—these media outlets can exploit that and tell you which version to believe…

So, I have concluded that each person has a version of the truth. Truth is not absolute for any of us, and I do believe that what we see is a reflection of how we *want* to see. In essence, we see what we want to see. If I believe Russia is to blame for the situation in the Ukraine, I will; and yet Russia Today's version of the truth is still truth—it's just someone else's version of it.

It is the same thing when we react to other people. If we can surrender our own ego and viewpoint and let go of our own conditioning and biases, then we can perhaps see our fellow humans simply as they truly are. In itself, this is an act of magic since it involves first changing ourselves in order to see more clearly—to see the divine spark in each and every person.

Part of our problem in trying to get along with one another, perhaps the entire problem, is that we have a habit of projecting ourselves onto those around us. When we interact with someone and dislike them, it's really because, in that person, we see the reflection of something we dislike or fear about ourselves.

We constantly measure others by projecting ourselves onto them. Our ego doesn't allow us to see this for what it really is. After all, I am an individual, separate, and by the way, I am surely superior. My views, my beliefs and my conditioning are used to synthesize and process my view of the other person, and I find them wanting in some way. Indeed, I may disagree with them and set them up as my 'enemy.'

If I know myself then I recognize my ego for what it truly is, and I place it to one side and tell it that I, the real me, I am in charge here! If I can learn to accept myself through self-knowing and coming to terms with who and what I really am, then I learn to love myself. In learning to love myself, I am able to love others through acceptance of what they are and where they are in their own journey.

Acceptance is the process of letting go, and as we let go, we no longer feel the need to struggle. We forgive ourselves, and we forgive others, and we learn how to truly love. It only when we truly know and love ourselves that we really gain the right and ability to guide others, knows how to help and correct without damaging that person's self-worth and progress. Otherwise, any act may be based on something less than love; it may be based on our distorted perspective of us.

This makes life really interesting. If there is no truth, then what am I to believe? Well, what is amazing is that if you do start to study magic or mysticism or your true self, you start to pick away at things, and like an onion, you find layer after layer of nonsense. You begin to understand that we are programmed and that our programming is continual, and we do not question it at all. You begin to see the world differently, but you accept that this view is not the truth but a different version of the truth as it is still viewed through the hue of the personality and the ego. The trick is to continually work at understanding yourself to minimize the tint that colors our observation.

At the same time, you must conclude that things that most people would not accept are not only feasible but probably can be made to be just by seeing the world in a different way—all it takes is rigorous practice. In other words, you begin to appreciate that magic is real and a lot more, besides. We do, in fact, create our own reality. It is a two-way thing. The way we see ensures that we continually see what we expect to see. If we change the lens, then we see something else. Is that magic or is that perception? And, please, what is the difference?

And this is where the fun really starts. As we do this, we become increasingly aware that there is a part of us—each of us—that is eternal, ever-present, all knowing and perfect in every way. Not only have we not known this before, but also if we did get a hint of it, then we dismissed it as a stupidity. But if we start to embrace this idea, then slowly, we begin to understand that if we just stand still in quiet and listen to this, our true self, we adopt a god-like viewpoint. In essence, we accept the will of God; and rather than trying to bend and strain to our program, we accept this… love. Then and only then will we finally see truth. The truth is you.

Ripples of Thought

In meditation, I often see ripples in a pool. They start at a point and move outwards as small waves. If the small wave meets an object, an interference pattern occurs.

Thoughts are like ripples. They start with a focus. Something triggers that focus, but then the thought expands like a ripple moving ever outwards into the world having that knows what impacts out there. Words—words are sounds, and sounds are waves; so when we speak, ripples move out from ourselves and those words can impact—not just those who hear them—but everything those sound ripples touch. Who knows what interference patterns result from our thoughts and words?

Those wave forms or ripples that we all create oscillate all around. Perhaps the smallest thought or word starts a ripple that becomes a tidal wave of change.

Silence. We are often instructed to be silent. And, if you think about it, with good reason for if our thoughts and words create ripples through the substratum of reality, then when we think or speak in anger, what effect does that have? Speech is a gift that we so often misuse and abuse. God help us if we could hear thoughts!

Think about it and contemplate what effect your ripples are having on reality.

A Conspiracy Mentality

I guess I have a bee in my bonnet about conspiracy theories. I find them funny, and those who chose to believe in them interesting. Today as I write this, the buzz on the net is all about the sudden and abrupt closing of five or six Wal-Mart stores across the southern US. The excuse used in all cases is plumbing problems and they are to be closed for six months. Well, Wal-Mart is the corporate Scrooge of all time, and there is no way plumbing problems would close any of their stores. Nope. Wal-Mart would do anything to keep its stores open. All of that is true. But what has this set of closings triggered? Well, here is a short list:

1. There is going to be a military exercise in the US in July or September 2015 codenamed Jade Helm. People are already making this out to be President Obama declaring martial law, and there are all kinds of weirdness being spouted on the net about it. Taking away Americans' guns is the favored one. I will bet it turns out to be just a military exercise, but don't quote me... Now, FEMA or some other part of the government, in cahoots with Wal-Mart, is going to use those stores to hold political prisoners and pro-gun US citizens will be held there...

2. A meteorite is going to strike the north of the US, and so the government is moving south and will use these stores for some re-staging capabilities (and multiple variations)

3. There will be a massive eruption on the NW coast and ditto as above

The list is actually endless, but those are my favourite three.

Apparently, these Wal-Marts were closed down, even filled with stock, and staff fired with five hours' notice. Sounds like typical Wal-Mart behavior to me...

The thing about conspiracy theorists is that they first develop a theory and then look for the evidence. Hundreds if not thousands of conspiracy theorists that see in it something sinister are seizing on Wal-Mart's actions. It never actually seems to enter their heads that any of the above list could be true and yet completely unrelated to Wal-Mart closures or any other event they 'collect' as evidence. There is no correlation either way and certainly no proof of anything, except perhaps that Wal-Mart is under severe pressure to close some stores from Wall St. Late last year, analysts pointed out that Wal-Mart's increasingly poor financial performance was probably due, in part, to the fact that it keeps opening larger and larger stores, but never shuts its smaller ones. Analysts are expecting Wal-Mart to close 100 under-performing stores, not just the six closures 'for plumbing reasons' that has caused this conspiracy storm.

The mind of a conspiracy theorist is a beautifully bizarre thing, isn't it? It's a total fixation on a particular theory to the point that any event can be deemed to support their distorted view of the world and reality.

But let's be honest with ourselves. Don't we all engage in such thinking at times in our lives? Don't we all convince ourselves that fate is against us, that we are unlucky or whatever, and then search for the evidence to support it? Don't we pile misery upon misery seeing insult and injustice where there was none just because we expect to? It's a thought, isn't it?

I certainly do that at times, and I am determined to eliminate my conspiracy thinking issues by not judging, but by expecting the very best, visualizing the very best and staying positive.

That way, I create a better reality.

I am no conspiracy theorist. I think that what things seem to be are mostly how they are. In my experience, if something can be cocked up and humans are involved, then it will be thoroughly cocked up. In other words, people who see deliberate acts of conspiracy are often really seeing cock-ups with no intention or pattern behind them. That's my view, anyway.

People who follow conspiracy theories begin to create a reality in which everything is a conspiracy. They believe, they see, and they make it so in their created world. They create that reality.

So, it is with certain other topics. I no longer pay much attention to the news because media is stupid, manipulated or both. Everyone has an agenda, and the aim of that agenda is to keep you fixated on the outer world, to keep you afraid and seeking others to protect you from your fears (i.e., giving them permission to enslave you). You see this in the fact that the media peddles out horror stories. This is bad for you that can give you cancer, the end of the world as we know it is nigh. Let's cut to the chase—this is largely nonsense. This is what I call 'myth making.' We cobble together some half-truth, take it out of context and publish it. Even better if a celebrity endorses it, too. But it is still myth.

I think to avoid falling into the mythmaker's trap; we all need to look for the balance. We need to reconcile the opposite points of view and seek the balance point. If there is truth, that is where we will find it. The best way to do this is not just to research and think about things, but also to meditate on them and consult the inner self. That's where you will find answers and the truth. If we all did this, then the power we grant the mythmakers to rule over us would disseminate and reality would change. The myths would become apparent to everyone. Perhaps, we would then suddenly find true freedom.

Taking Back Responsibility

As an esotericist, I have come to the conclusion that I am responsible for myself. I have half an idea that for many new agers and the like, this statement is akin to saying I am a Satanist, but I stand by my statement, nonetheless. We all create our reality—this place in which we live. We create it in the way that we see things and how we act. Thoughts are things, and they manifest as reality. Only I can create my reality, therefore, I am responsible for my thoughts and what they create. As a self-responsible co-creator of this reality we live in, I must strive to improve myself. I don't mean make more money or buy a bigger house. No, I mean improve myself spiritually, and as I do so, the changes in my thinking, perceptions and actions will help to co-create a better reality.

Today, too many people are here for the ride. They seem to believe that they are owed a life and not just that, but a good life. They look to others to take responsibility for their lives, too. In part, the system creates this codependency as we now fail to educate or even value education. We fail to value charity as well. In the USA, the whole system was based on the freedom to build a life and then pay society back through charity, but the do-gooders want a safety net. They want the wealthy to pay and forget charity. They want a socialist utopia that fails and will fail because it creates dependency. It erodes the idea of taking responsibility for self-improvement. It enslaves people to misery by having them rely on others to create reality.

These days, there are so many people cheating the system. Collecting benefits by fraud, not paying taxes by dealing in cash, not issuing receipts to avoid VAT, cheating on expenses and so on. There is this pervasive sense of *'I must get ahead at any cost'* and it crosses social and political dividing lines, too. This erosion of moral values is another facet of the idea that 'I am not responsible' – someone else is. It is all about understanding that each and every one of us is personally responsible for own actions and behavior. If we cheat the system, then we are contributing to a reality in which it's okay to cheat your neighbor and in which others will emulate.

I often hear people say, "Well, I have no choice because the system is a certain way." It may very well be, but that doesn't give you an exception from accepting personal responsibility for your life and actions! In essence, if you don't accept personal responsibility then you are simply just another manipulated and semi-conscious sheep.

If we are to improve our communal lot, it isn't through leveling the playing field, punishing successful people, rewarding sloth and laziness with unnecessary benefits, idolizing the useless (sports people, actors, singers, etc.) while penalizing the talented (teachers, nurses, etc.). No, we must continually remind ourselves that we must all accept personal responsibility, not just for ourselves, but for the reality we all live in. We must seek to improve ourselves so that we improve the whole. We must learn that true love of our fellow man isn't giving them something for nothing and making them more dependent. No, it's teaching them self-respect and how to accept responsibility.

Am I Really Thinking at All?

Around 95% of our brain activity is said to be the unconscious mind. That means I am only 5% conscious.

If this is true, and I have no doubt that it is, what does it actually mean? The subconscious mind is like a tape recorder where I can set up a bunch of activities and then run it over and over again. It's a sort of set of automated routines running in background that maintains bodily functions and habits. It is also often our adversary.

Through my mind, I create my reality. But if 95% of my thoughts are subconscious and I am unaware of them or they are accidentally or purposely programmed responses like fear and flight, my reality will be chaotic and might even become a total nightmare. One thing I have done very well is to build up responses, roles and actors all managed by my subconscious mind. These all play out without much interaction from me.

I have written before that we often react to people based on ourselves. The things we hate about ourselves are reflected back at us, and we don't like what we see. We dislike people because they remind us deep down of the qualities, we do not like within ourselves. We blame everyone and everything for our problems as a subconscious avoidance mechanism. What is it we are avoiding? Ourselves.

I also often say we have to accept responsibility for ourselves. To some, this is a cold-hearted politically motivated statement; but actually, it is the truth people seek. If WE create our own reality through our thoughts and deeds and if we project our subconscious desires and worries onto the world around us, then WE are responsible. No one else but us. We have to take personal responsibility for our lives and ourselves. This is not political—it is a fact of reality. Perhaps I could restate it differently by saying that we need to become more conscious of who we are, why we are and work to improve and take more control as the real people we are inside. That is accepting personal responsibility. As opposed to being political, it is a spiritual act.

This is where meditation and working to know oneself comes in. It's not good enough, though, to scrape the surface. We must face our demons or else we project them out to the external world and into the reality that we create. We must forgive ourselves for being human before we can forgive those around us as well. We must resolve the duality or polarity inside of us in order to dissolve its effects in our reality.

The External World

The external world presents us with a constant barrage of noise. The messages flood in subliminally all of the time via advertisements, political and religious messages. Much of this we do not consciously notice, but knowing how the subconscious mind works, the clever people who want us to behave in ways that suit them use our minds against us. They know that we sleep through our lives and can be programmed continually. It is almost impossible to escape from their influences.

But you can, you should, and here is how….

Steps to Creating Your Own Reality

From today on, you will live your life differently. Over time, you will begin to notice that coincidences occur all of the time and that things that you WANT manifest themselves in your life with increasing frequency. It will take time and practice. It will take effort. Change will occur, though, if you follow these concepts and exercises.

Daily Meditation

Firstly, you must learn to meditate, and you must take the time to meditate daily for reasonable lengths of time (twenty minutes or more daily). You should buy a notebook, and immediately following meditation, write down any thoughts, images or feelings for future reference.

According to Wikipedia, meditation can be defined as "a state of concentrated attention on some object of thought or awareness. It usually involves turning the attention inward to a single point of reference."

For me, meditation involves reaching a state known as 'mind awake, body asleep.' Several techniques may then be used to actually meditate including constant thought and attention on an object, symbol or a statement; or, my favored approach, emptying of the mind to simply let images arise that are noted and then dismissed. I will discuss these two approaches in more detail later.

To meditate properly, that is, to reach the correct state of 'body asleep, mind awake,' is in fact quite difficult. Some students have immense problems getting there at all. The key, however, to reaching such a state is relaxation.

Relaxation

Trying to truly relax in today's hectic life can be very difficult, but we all do manage it every night as we fall asleep. Unless one can enter a truly relaxed state, is it difficult and arguably impossible to meditate, and for that reason a lot of writers on the subject have spent a great deal of time talking about relaxation.

To properly relax and prepare for a state of meditation, one must obviously remove oneself from all distractions. What is needed is a quiet location where one will be undisturbed. Some people set aside a room or a space exactly for this purpose away from TVs, other people and telephones. Some might seek an outdoor location that has a beautiful and peaceful view. Whatever your approach, it is key to find a location that to you is serene, peaceful and where you are unlikely to be disturbed.

Two approaches to relaxation work effectively for me and will be discussed here. Both involve adopting a sitting position with a straight backbone although the head can be dropped forward resting the chin on the top of the breast. The best and most effective position is one in which you sit in a comfortable chair with both feet placed on the floor, your back straight and your hands placed one on each leg. Initially, this might feel uncomfortable, but it is the best position for a number of reasons.

Progressive Relaxation

The first approach uses a stepwise and progressive conscious method to relaxation. First, adopting the meditation position described above, take several slow and deep breaths. Initially, one can count mentally as follows: breathe in slowly and deeply (one-two-three), breathe out slowly and deeply (one-two-three). You can vary the count according to what feels comfortable. However, maintain this breathing for up to a minute until it becomes rhythmic and almost second nature.

Next, starting with the toes of each foot in turn, imagine that they are becoming totally relaxed. All tension in those toes is slowly disappearing and they are beginning to simply 'float.' When you feel that this is achieved, concentrate similarly on your feet, next your legs up to the kneecap and so on all the way up your body until you finally reach your neck and head, which will naturally flop onto your breast as described above.

Now check that all parts of your body are totally relaxed. You might feel now as if you are floating as opposed to sitting, and if so, that's good. Your body should be completely relaxed. Now, you must keep it that way and that means quite often that you must quiet your mind. Try to stop all thinking and just be. If a thought pops into your head—suppress it immediately and empty your mind again. It's good enough to simply practice this over a period of a few weeks until it becomes second nature before even starting to try to meditate. If you are successful, not only will it feel as if you are floating, but you will also lose all impression of your body and become 'mind awake, body asleep.'

The Liquid Method

A second approach is to adopt the same position, but this time imagine that there is a way to pour liquid into your body at the top of your head and another valve at the base of your feet that can be used to empty the liquid out again. Now, imagine that a tank of green liquid is being poured into your body until this green liquid fills every part of your entire body. For a while, sit there knowing that your body is filled with green liquid—that liquid is clear and beautiful, and it attracts stress. You will now begin to imagine and feel all the stress in your body start to come out of your body as the green liquid does its work. See the green liquid turn slowly cloudy and reddish-brown as the stress enters it from your body and feel how relaxed you are becoming in the process. When the liquid seems very reddish-brown and very cloudy, unlock the valve at your feet and let it pour away. Feel your body relaxing throughout this process and repeat it several times.

Staying Relaxed

While these are my two preferred methods, it should be noted that there are many other methods that can be used, and you need to find the one that works for you. Once relaxed, the next issue is staying relaxed. The key is to make sure that you won't be disturbed and to stay sort of empty-headed as long as possible. However, if you start to tense up or lose the state of relaxation, don't worry too much. Just focus again on relaxing, and remember, this takes practice and patience.

Having learned how to relax and found a suitable location where you will not be disturbed, the next phase in meditation is the actual meditation itself. In general, there are two or perhaps three methods of meditating:

- Focus on a word, phrase, image and drill down into it
- Keep the mind blank and allow images to arise
- Guided meditation (also known as 'Pathworking')

Let's look at each in turn.

Focused Meditation

In focused meditation, we already know what it is we wish to meditate on. It can be a useful technique when you want to examine something and really drill down into it. An example is perhaps the better way to examine focused meditation. We have read a book and enjoyed it, but it really made us think. We decide to meditate and take a key phrase, thought or viewpoint from the book as our area of focus. Having relaxed, we begin to meditate in our mind awake, body asleep state by simply taking that phrase and examining it. In a sense, this is active meditation because we actively work on the phrase. During this process, thoughts will arise, and those thoughts can be followed if they appear to be on target or dismissed if not. It's like drilling for oil—this active, focused technique as we drill into the phrase or words. Images might arise, other words and phrases might come to mind, but we stay focused constantly drilling down into the substance, the ideas, and the meanings of the phrase.

Active meditation is used by many occult schools to both train the mind and to enable you to extract value from within yourself about the topic of study. It is hard work and requires constant focus and re-focus of the mind on the task at hand. It can, however, be very rewarding.

Here is a personal example. I decided to meditate upon the subject of fire. My approach was to imagine sitting on a beach in front of a driftwood fire and actually see the flames, hear the crackling, smell the smoke and feel the heat on my face. While doing this visualization, I kept asking, "What is fire?" After a while, it seemed that I became the fire and I became a flame. In that instant, I knew what it was to be fire, what my needs were and how I was. Too hard to explain in words, but the technique worked, and I hope the example provides some insight as to how this approach might work.

Empty Minded Meditation

Maybe I am just lazy, but this is my favorite approach to meditation. Rather than focus on anything, you empty and still the mind. You do not allow any thought to enter but simply stay focused on an empty mind. I don't know why I believe this to be a lazy approach because it is very difficult to achieve. Imagine not thinking for any length of time.

Nonetheless, if you are successful, you will find that at some point, images well up inside the mind and you begin a journey as if in a dream. Again, an example: Once when I used this technique, I saw a pipe extruding from a mud cliff. Out of the pipe streamed water, and I followed the water into the ocean where I became one with the ocean and everything in it. It was like being inside a dream but awake, and in a real sense I could control how the dream unfolded. Go anywhere, do anything.

Guided Meditation

Pathworking or Guided Meditation has become much more popular in recent years. The technique here also involves the ability to visualize. On entering a meditative state, one essentially listens to a taped account of the guided meditation or narrative and you follow along, allowing the guided meditation to drag you along in images in your mind. Again, this is quite difficult and requires practice but can produce astounding results. The best way to do a guided meditation is to tape yourself slowly reading the text of the guided meditation and to sit there with headphones on and play it back to yourself.

What's Next?

To really get the most out of meditation one must—absolutely must—write down immediately afterwards your impressions. Like dreams, meditational experiences drift away quite quickly in normal consciousness, and if you don't write it down, it is lost to you. If you write down your experiences, over time, you may see patterns emerge or a trend develop. Try it and you will see....

Some Warnings

A few things NOT to do...

1. Try not to be disturbed. If you suddenly come out of a meditational state because the phone is ringing or something, it can be quite a shock.
2. After completing the meditation session, take some time to come back down to earth. Stamp your feet or something and be sure you are really completely awake. Once, I stood up immediately after a session and promptly fell and hit my head as my legs gave way...

3. Don't try too hard. This sounds strange but do stay relaxed and patient. Trying too hard somehow seems to get us all tense again.

What to Meditate On

Initially, you will meditate on yourself. You will examine yourself under a microscope. You will think about your faults, your strengths and what you believe about your world. You will begin to break down the programming and conditioning that you have been subjected to all of your life. Think about your conspiracy theories and how they stop you from achieving your objectives. Think about your expectations and what you give your attention to and why. Write your findings down and work on these issues in any way that you can including using some of the methods below.

Next, you will meditate on what you want for yourself. Dream a little. Visualize yourself being successful, getting all the things that you ever wanted. See yourself happy doing what you want to do and exploring the reality that you are making for yourself. Think and visualize yourself giving attention to the things you want to and not what you are told to or driven to through fear mongering or subconscious direction. See yourself accepting responsibility for your own life, your own actions and your own future.

In these sessions, you must learn to visualize and hone your imagination. Don't just see it—feel it, smell it, touch it. It is so real in your mind that it is real. Daydream a bit and imagine how you would feel, what it would be like to be what you want. Feel it, be it, and act it. In fact, top athletes who pay small fortunes to coaches to help them visualize winning use this approach.

Next, pray. Yes, you heard me. Pray. But don't stream a bunch of meaningless words, not thinking about what it is you are saying. No, imagine and visualize what you are praying about as hard as you are able. See what you are praying about and for and be thankful for what you already have.

When you awaken or go to sleep, tell yourself over and over again in your mind a simple positive statement like, "I am successful." Do it forty or sixty times and try to do it when you are sleepy or only half-awake. You are programming your subconscious with positive affirmations about yourself. Equally, use other opportunities to reprogram yourself. Imagine that the water in the shower is washing away your negative qualities and visualize your food and drink as giving you not just sustenance, but also the success that you deserve.

Finally, act the way that you want to be. Have faith and confidence in yourself. By behaving the way that you want to be, you will change your reality. What I mean is: act as if you already have what it is you want.

In the end, you must spend many hours unteaching yourself that you are a failure or that you don't deserve happiness. You must dig deep and find the real you in order to know what will make you happy. Be warned—it may not be wealth and big houses when you get right down to it! You must then reprogram yourself with positive messages and affirmations and expectations. Expect and give your attention sparingly to just those things that you want to bring into reality. Quit watching the news and reading the papers and quit arguing politics or religion. Be you. Express yourself. Be realistic and create your life step-by-step the way you desire it to be.

Remember what I said at the beginning of this book:

- We must be consistent and willful in setting up what is it is that we want to create,

- We must remain disciplined and focused on that objective unwavering in its pursuit,
- We must also have the clarity of mind to stay focused and a powerful imagination to actually see and feel it around us,
- We must know ourselves and be in tune with our Higher Self in order to align what we think we want with what we actually need,
- Identify your conspiracy theory and stop seeing life as a set of events that agrees with that,
- Thoughts are things—energy follows your attention,
- Subconscious mind is your enemy—make it your friend,

Create a great reality!

If you enjoyed this book, please do leave a review and perhaps check out some of my other books ….

Other Books by G. Michael Vasey

The Chilling True Terror of the Black Eyed Kids: A Monster Compilation, Asteroth's Books, 2017 (Compilation of The Black Eyed Kids and The Black Eyed Demons Are Coming)
ASIN: B075FVSMB3
Kindle and paperback

Lord of the Elements, Asteroth's Books, 2017 (fiction)
ASIN: B072M4PD68
Kindle and paperback

Poltergeist: True, Terrifying Tales of the Noisy Ghost, Asteroth's Books, 2017
ASIN: B072KDZ2WJ
Kindle version

Ghosts of the Living, Asteroth's Books, 2017
ASIN: B06XWSK4C9
Kindle version

Paranormal Eyewitness: True Accounts to Keep You Awake Tonight, Asteroth's Books, 2017 (Your Haunted Lives and Your Haunted Lives Revisited Compilation)
ASIN: B06WRTXZPW
Kindle and paperback versions

The Black-Eyed Demons Are Coming, Asteroth's Books, 2017
ASIN: B06X9BJMNC
Kindle version only

True Tales of haunted Places, Asteroth's Books, 2016
ASIN: B01MQQIC3C
Kindle and audiobook

The Czech Republic – The Most Haunted Country in the World? Asteroth's Books, 2016
ASIN: B01LXJ78PV
Kindle and paperback

Black Eyed Kids: Can We Come in? Asteroth's Books, 2016
ASIN: B01K02OH9W
Kindle and audio books

Your Haunted Lives Revisited, Asteroth's Books, 2016
ASIN: B01ENXOINO
Kindle and audio books

The Pink Bus: Amazing Paranormal Encounters after Death (fiction), Asteroth's Books, 2016
ASIN: B01CZUBO1Q
Kindle and audio book versions

Shades of A Haunted Life – a Sampler, Asteroth's Books, 2016
ASIN: B01BGV36RU
Kindle version

Your Haunted Lives, Asteroth's Books, 2016
ASIN: B01A7RJ934
Kindle and audio book versions

The Mystical Hexagram: The Seven Inner Stars of Power (with SC Vincent), Asteroth's Books, 2015
ASIN: B016SIV6LY
Paperback and Kindle Versions

Death on the Beach, Asteroth's Books, 2015 (Poetry)
ASIN: B015ZB1C7I
Kindle Only
Ghosts in The Machines, Asteroth's Books, 2015
ASIN: B013Y3QMCY

Kindle and audio book versions

God's Pretenders: Incredible True Stories of Magic and Sorcery, Asteroth's Books, 2015
ASIN: B00W21D1F6
E-book and audio book versions

My Haunted Life – Extreme Edition, Ronin Robot Press, 2015
ISBN: 0986087351
Paperback, audio book and Kindle versions

The Art of Science, Asteroth's Books, 2015 (Poetry)
ASIN: B00TIKYXEW
ISBN: 978-1508460541
Paperback, Kindle and Audio book versions

My Haunted Life 3, William Collins Publishing, 2015
ASIN: B00RN3KO94
E-book and audio book versions

My Haunted Life Too, William Collins Publishing, London, 2014
ASIN: B00QSY6H6S
E-book and audio book

My Haunted Life – A Compendium of Strange (But True) Tales of the Paranormal, William Collins Publishing, London, 2014
ISBN: 1503041824
E-book and audio book versions

Best Laid Plans and Other Strange Tails, BookSurge, 2014 (Poetry)
ISBN: 1500889601
Paperback and Kindle Versions

Moon Whispers, BookSurge, 2014 (Poetry)

ISBN: 1499364105
Paperback and Kindle versions

Poems for the Little Room (Reissued), BookSurge, 2014 (Poetry)
ISBN: 1493783114
Paperback and Kindle versions.

Astral Messages, BookSurge, 2013 (Poetry)
ISBN: 1490312633
Paperback and Kindle Formats

The Last Observer: A Magical Battle for Reality, Roundfire, 2013 (Fiction)
ISBN: 1782791825
Paperback and all formats of eBook

Weird Tales: Other World Poetry, Booksurge, 2006 (Poetry)
ISBN: 141965277X
Paperback and Kindle versions

About the Author

G. Michael Vasey is a Yorkshire man and rabid Tigers fan that has spent most of his adult life lost deep in Texas and more lately, in the Czech Republic. While lucky enough to write for a living as a leading analyst in the commodity trading and risk management industry, he surreptitiously writes strange poems and equally strange books and stories on the topics of metaphysics, the occult and the paranormal on the side, hoping that one-day, someone might actually buy them.

After growing up experiencing ghosts, poltergeist and other strange and scary experiences, he developed an interest in magic and the esoteric. These days he fancies himself as a bit of a mystic and a magician to boot. Most of his inspiration for his scribbling comes from either meditation or occasionally, very loud heavy metal music.

He has appeared on radio shows such as Everyday Connection and X Radio with Rob McConnell to tell strange and scary stories. He has also been featured in Chat - Its Fate magazine and interviewed by Ghost Village and Novel Ideas amongst others.

He blogs addictively at garymvasey.com.

He also reviews a lot of very weird books at strangebookreviews.com.

Printed in Great Britain
by Amazon